Original title:
Wildwood Woes and Wonders

Copyright © 2025 Creative Arts Management OÜ
All rights reserved.

Author: Theodore Sinclair
ISBN HARDBACK: 978-1-80567-320-0
ISBN PAPERBACK: 978-1-80567-619-5

Orchard of Unheard Whispers

In the orchard, fruits get shy,
They giggle as the squirrels fly by.
Apples claim they have a dream,
To roll downhill and start a team.

Bananas wave with yellow glee,
As pears just dangle, carefree.
Cherries laugh with silly flair,
While grapefruits juggle in mid-air.

Ancestral Echoes in the Timber

In the woods, old trees will tease,
With whispers carried on the breeze.
Acorns drop with quite a plop,
As elder trunks gossip and swap.

Squirrels chuckle in a twist,
Over things that they insist:
"My grandpa saw a fox that danced,
But it tripped—oh, how we pranced!"

Through the Eyes of Wistful Creatures

Beneath the ferns, a rabbit sighs,
He envies how the birdbirds fly.
With floppy ears and dreams unbound,
He hops around the silent ground.

A hedgehog grins with spiny cheer,
As fireflies twinkle, drawing near.
"Let's make a band!" he starts to shout,
But all his friends just roll about.

Reflections on a Mossy Stone

On a stone where moss does grow,
A frog contemplates the show.
With bulging eyes, he sings aloud,
"Why can't we jump like cats so proud?"

Tadpoles swirl in water's dance,
Each one hoping for a chance.
But dodging flies, they laugh and pout,
"Just watch us leap, no doubt—we're stout!"

Soliloquy of the Silver Streams

A fish in a suit swam by with flair,
He waved with a fin, as if he cared.
Bubbles popped like tiny balloons,
Laughing at turtles and their afternoon tunes.

A frog on a lily pad, quite the sight,
Wore a crown made of twigs, say what a fright!
He croaked of adventures, both silly and grand,
While ants threw a party, quite unplanned.

Footprints in the Fading Light

The sun gave a wink, then hid with a grin,
As shadows danced lightly, let the fun begin.
A rabbit in specs read a book by the glow,
The plot thickened fast, the characters row.

Squirrels played chess with acorns for stakes,
While deer gossip gleefully, making mistakes.
The night crept in, but laughter stayed bright,
In a world full of giggles, embraced by the night.

The Call of the Hidden Hollow

There's a secret nook where the daisies tease,
Giggling behind leaves in a playful breeze.
A snail in a race, no hurry in sight,
Chuckled with crickets about their plight.

At dusk, the owls wore hats made of cheese,
Hosting a banquet with muffins and peas.
The fireflies twinkled like stars in dismay,
As raccoons in tuxedos started their play.

Tales from the Canvas of Green

Beneath the tall brush, a bear danced with pride,
To a tune played by bees, all swarming beside.
Grasshoppers hummed in a jazzy affair,
While lizards in bowties flaunted their flair.

The wind whispered secrets, giggles ensued,
Flowers rolled over with laughter, quite rude.
As twilight laid down its colorful dreams,
The meadow became a stage of wild schemes.

Visions in the Misty Woods

In the mist, I see a mouse,
Looking for crumbs, in my house.
He wears a hat that's far too big,
And dances like a tiny pig.

A squirrel swings on branches high,
Chasing shadows as they fly.
He trips and tumbles, what a scene!
That nut was quite the trampoline!

A rabbit hops with flair so grand,
Pretending he can make a stand.
But every leap's a comic slip,
He lands right in a puddle's grip.

The trees giggle, their leaves applaud,
As antics tumble, quite a fraud.
Nature's stage is set tonight,
With laughter echoing in the light.

The Solace of Crumbling Bark

Oh, the trees that whisper low,
Sharing secrets only they know.
But while they chat, I start to snooze,
And wake to find I've missed the cues.

The bark is rough, it scratches my back,
A wooden hug, but what a hack!
I step and trip, a clumsy oaf,
Wishing I had brought a loaf!

The mushrooms giggle, hats askew,
They've thrown a party, just for you.
But stepping close, I start to slide,
And there I go, in laugh-incide!

The squirrels throw acorns like confetti,
While I try to dance, but I'm unsteady.
Nature chuckles at my plight,
As crumbling bark hugs me tight.

A Symphony of Twisting Vines

In the garden, vines entwine,
Playing music, oh so fine.
But one decided to play a prank,
Knotted my shoelaces, how charming, bank!

The birds above join in the tune,
Chirping loudly, a merry boon.
Yet one dove in, with flair and style,
And landed right on my head for a while.

A crabapple fell with a squish, squish, squish,
Turning my pants into a mushy wish.
The vines now laugh at my mishap,
As ants parade around, ready to clap.

And while I'm tangled, caught in strings,
The forest sways and freely sings.
A symphony that brightens the day,
With laughter echoing, come what may.

The Memory of a Silent Clearing

In a clearing bright and wide,
I found a place where I could hide.
But oh, the grass was tickling me,
A secret, soft, but oh so free!

The stones sat quiet, wearing moss,
But one rolled over, what a boss!
Giggling stones, who knew they could?
They tumbled down, as stones all would.

The butterflies performed their dance,
Each flutter, just a crazy chance.
But when they landed, I sneezed loud,
Scattering them like a silly cloud!

The trees stood witness, roots aglow,
As I tried to bow, but tripped, oh no!
Yet in this silence, joy did bloom,
My awkwardness brought laughter's room.

The Gnarled Roots of Time

In the twist of roots, they argue loud,
A squirrel jokes, all feels so proud.
The owl hoots back with a sage-like frown,
Who knew wisdom wore a feathery crown?

The ants march in line, a very fine troop,
Stumbling on mushrooms, all fall in a loop.
Nature's court jesters, they trip and they dash,
While a hedgehog laughs, 'Now that's quite the crash!'

Flickering Fireflies and Fractured Hopes

A firefly flicks with a wobbly glow,
'Hey, watch me dance!' a big bug says, 'Whoa!'
The hopes they hold like lanterns bright,
Only to crash into a wrong flight.

'Why so dim?' asked the moon, feeling bold,
'We're waiting on dreams that never unfold.'
They blink and they giggle in twilight's embrace,
Lost in their world, now this is their place.

Veils of Mist in the Forest Depths

Through the mist, a tree whispers, 'Careful, my child.'
A clumsy young deer, startled and wild.
"I swear I saw something," it bleats in fright,
But it's just a raccoon, lounging all night.

The fog wraps the trees in a soft, silly hug,
While a snail in its shell, laughs and gives a shrug.
'What's the rush?' it wonders, 'Just enjoy the view,'
But then it sees a worm, and off it flew!

The Resilient Heart of Nature

A little old flower peeks through the stone,
'You think I'm fragile? Just watch me grown!'
With petals like laughter and roots deep in cheer,
It giggles at clouds that dare disappear.

The trees hold a meeting, their branches all sway,
'Let's plan a party, we'll dance all day!'
The chairs are just mushrooms, the drinks are sweet dew,
And all of the critters shout, 'Count me in too!'

Enigma of the Enchanted Grove

In a grove where whispers play,
The trees dance in a wobbly way.
Squirrels wear hats, quite absurd,
And gossip like they've lost their word.

A frog with boots jumps on a log,
Reciting poetries to a dog.
The mushrooms chuckle, round and wide,
While bees in coats take a joyride.

Mystery lurks in every nook,
Like the owl who's writing a book.
Elves giggle behind a leaf,
Climbing high with no belief.

The grass whispers jokes, oh so sly,
While leaves perform a silly fly.
Nature's laughter fills the air,
With trees that wiggle, unaware.

Lament of the Bursting Buds

Buds burst forth in wild dismay,
Cheerful blooms in a bright ballet.
Yet a butterfly flutters by,
With a sneeze that makes it cry.

The petals giggle, trying to sway,
As raindrops tap and play their way.
A ladybug hums a tune,
While tulips argue with the moon.

Each flower's tale is quite a jest,
Of overconfidence at best.
Beehives buzz with absurd delight,
As pollen stumbles into flight.

But oh, the garden's meltdown spree,
Where all the colors clash to flee.
In chaos, joy does intertwine,
And bursts of laughter bloom in line.

Shadows Over the Glade

In a glade where shadows creep,
The gnomes have secrets they won't keep.
With hats too big, they try to hide,
But trip on roots, a giddy ride.

Owls snicker from their lofty seat,
While rabbits scamper with twinkling feet.
A fox tells jokes, so grand and sly,
That even the stars crack up in the sky.

Fog rolls in like a fluffy blanket,
Hiding creatures who love to prank it.
The moonlight giggles on the ground,
As shadows dance, both lost and found.

Even the night plays tricks with glee,
With flickering lights on the old pine tree.
In this glade where laughter's grand,
Every shadow takes a stand.

Mysteries of the Twilight Thicket

In the twilight thicket, secrets reign,
Each branch recites a silly chain.
A hedgehog juggles acorns neat,
While the crickets dance on nimble feet.

Twinkling lights wink in disguise,
As fireflies plot their comic rise.
The moon wears spectacles, quite the sight,
Debating jokes with the starry night.

Bamboo whispers riddles so odd,
As raccoons play a game of God.
With hats made of leaves, they take the stage,
Performing antics that amuse the sage.

In this thicket, the weird thrives,
With creatures living their jolly dives.
It's a riot of fun in every nook,
Where mischief glances from every book.

Whispers of the Untamed Forest

In the thicket, where squirrels tease,
Their chatter travels in the breeze.
A chipmunk juggles acorns with glee,
While rabbits dance, wild and free.

The owls hoot jokes upon the boughs,
While clever foxes take their bows.
A raccoon sneaks a late-night snack,
As fireflies light up the track.

Trees whisper secrets, oh so sly,
To each wandering creature nearby.
A bear with style wears a hat,
And claims he's busy, just like that!

With nature's giggles all around,
Life's a circus without a sound.
Each creature plays their merry part,
In the forest, wild heart to heart.

Shadows of Forgotten Pines

In shadows deep, where jokes abound,
Old trees groan with a creaky sound.
A beetle waltzes, quite the sight,
While crickets argue 'til the night.

Pinecones knock like drums of fate,
As sloths declare, they're running late.
A squirrel slips on a mossy mat,
And lands right next to a sneaky cat.

The sun peeks through with a cheeky grin,
And nudges all the fun to begin.
A wise old owl has lost his specs,
He's flapping 'round, what silly wrecks!

In this grove, laughter rings out loud,
Nature's antics form quite the crowd.
Where shadows play tricks and pines do sway,
Funny moments brighten the day.

Echoes in the Canopy

Among the trees, echoes of mirth,
Where mischief rules, and laughs give birth.
A parrot jokes, "What's a tree's name?"
"Bark Twain!" it squawks, a pun in fame.

High above, adventurous birds,
Share the funniest of the nerds.
A woodpecker drumming in delight,
Says, "I just wanted to take flight!"

Down below, the mushrooms giggle,
As rabbits hop, then do a wiggle.
A deer insists on having a dance,
While bushes blush at the glance.

In laughter's realm, the wild comes alive,
Creatures embrace each silly jive.
The canopy sings with joy and cheer,
In this merry dance, we all draw near.

Secrets Beneath the Leafy Veil

Under leaves, where shadows dwell,
A mouse spins tales, oh so swell.
He whispers secrets soft and sweet,
While frogs provided the funky beat.

A turtle hums, moving slow,
Says "Life's a race, but I won't go!"
A wiggly worm joins in the fun,
With moves that leave the crowd undone.

The hedgehogs argue who's cuter still,
As ants march home with a hearty meal.
The bramble thickets hide and seek,
In playful chaos, laughter's peak.

From roots to crowns, knowledge grows,
In nature's play, everyone knows.
With secrets kept beneath the trees,
This wild family laughs with ease.

Ghosts of the Green Canopy

In the trees where the squirrels chatter,
A ghost once spilled tea, it was quite the matter.
With a crumpet in hand, he did a jig,
And scared a bold rabbit who ran off too big.

Leaves flutter like ghosts in a sarcastic dance,
Twirling and swirling, they took a chance.
A raccoon laughed loud at the specter's plight,
While owls rolled their eyes, it was quite a sight.

"Boo!" said the ghost, with a feigned bravado,
While the hedgehog just snored, feeling quite like a despot.
But then came a breeze, and with it a twist,
The ghost lost his grip—oh, who could resist?

"Gotcha!" cried a fox, as he leaped from the brush,
With a bark and a laugh, causing quite the hush.
In the canopy thick, where the laughter still flows,
You'll find that the haunt is less fright than it shows!

Trails of Forgotten Bloodlines

Down the path where the old boots lay,
Ancestors squabble in a comical fray.
A moose in a top hat took a bow,
While a badger sung ballads, singing "Meow!"

Shade of the trees offers whispers so strange,
A riddle from grandpa that's hard to exchange.
"Who's the bravest?" they ask, with sprouts in the fray,
But the tortoise just chuckles and goes on his way.

They argue and bicker as shadows stretch long,
About all their feats, oh, the tales they prolong.
Yet when it's time for a joyous feast,
They forget all their squabbles, and dance like the least!

So if you meander down this winding lane,
And hear ghostly laughter, don't sip at the rain.
Just join in the jigs and the silliness too,
For trails of old laughter belong to you!

Harbingers of Untamed Seasons

In springtime, a fox wore a daffodil crown,
With a prance and a wink, he strutted through town.
"Look at me, darlings!" he laughed with delight,
While the daisies all giggled, oh what a sight!

Summer arrived with the sun shining bright,
A bear tried to swim, but oh, what a fright!
He flopped like a fish with a belly so round,
And the frogs laughed so hard, they fell to the ground.

Autumn brought pumpkins that rolled down the street,
Ghosts in the orchard danced hopping on feet.
A squirrel yelled, "Catch that round pumpkin surprise!"
And they all tumbled over, in fits of goodbyes!

Then winter, with snowflakes that danced in the air,
The moose donned a scarf, snorting without care.
They laugh at the seasons, in quirky, odd shows,
These harbingers silly, where laughter still grows!

The Forgotten Tales of the Earth

In the forest, trees gossip loud,
Squirrels tell secrets, feeling proud.
A raccoon winks, with a wild claim,
He once rode a bike in the evening game.

Mushrooms throw parties, dancing with glee,
Toadstool hats worn by a bug or three.
The roots chuckle, oh what a sight,
As shadows do tango in the moonlight.

The lost socks wander, mismatched and bold,
Singing to crickets, forgetting the cold.
The breeze whispers jokes, a gentle tease,
While owls laugh softly at the rustling leaves.

Thus tales unfurl, bizarre yet bright,
Nature's laughter echoes through the night.
In this curious place, humor takes flight,
Where woodland creatures showcase their delight.

A Journey Through Gnarled Paths

With every step, roots trip my feet,
The path is twisted, nothing elite.
A hedgehog snorts, in such fine style,
Claiming he'll run a marathon in a while.

The trees lean in, gossiping fast,
While shadows dance, they were once vast.
A squirrel's complaint echoes with flair,
Claiming acorns are totally unfair.

A deer slips by, with a wink and nod,
Wearing a crown of the most odd sod.
The brambles chuckle, they like to tease,
While mocking the lost, with absurd ease.

Through tangled tales, wild chaos spills,
In laughter and jests, the forest fills.
Every twisted turn brings a surprise,
Nature's joke book never complies.

Portraits of Silence in the Woods

In the hush of trees, a beetle croons,
He's got some rhythm, for late night tunes.
A fox poses grand, just like a star,
Wearing a cape made from leaves near and far.

The quiet builds a theater show,
Where crickets play lead with a gentle glow.
If trees could giggle, oh what a sound,
As laughter of silence wraps all around.

Mice take the stage, performing with grace,
In tiny top hats, they pick up the pace.
Nature's portraits brush with a wink,
In the gentlest whispers, we dare not blink.

So sit and absorb, this serene wild ball,
Where the silence sings, enchanting us all.
A world quite quirky in dusky embrace,
Each moment a giggle, in this sacred space.

In the Embrace of Twilight's Veil

As dusk falls gently, giggles arise,
Fireflies play tag beneath the skies.
The raccoon sneaks snacks, plotting a feast,
While a wise old owl gives a hearty tease.

Under the twilight, shadows come alive,
With hues of laughter, they twist and jive.
A hedgehog's got moves, oh what a show,
Stealing the spotlight, stealing the glow.

Blabbering branches share tales of old,
Of chilly nights and adventures bold.
Each rustle a punchline, gently told,
While the stars above twinkle, bright and gold.

In this whimsical eve, all creatures play,
With a sprinkle of mischief to chase fears away.
Forever in jest, the twilight's reprieve,
Holds laughter encased in the webs we weave.

Remnants of Lamented Seasons

A squirrel with a plaid cap, style so bright,
Pauses to ponder, is it day or night?
He flips through the leaves, chasing his dream,
But winds whip around, making him scream!

The acorns he hoards, a treasure so grand,
But every nut's missing; it's just his own hand.
With a twirl and a tumble, he sets off again,
To find bits of autumn, or trouble, or grain.

A fox in a coat, the color of cheese,
Wanders through shadows, with admirable ease.
He sneezes through pine and causes a scene,
The forest erupts, it's a laugh so keen.

With whispers of winter, the grass starts to freeze,
But here in the wild, we do as we please.
So let's raise a toast, with a leaf in our hand,
To memories made in this magical land!

The Last Dance of Autumn Leaves

The trees with their hats, all swirled out of sight,
Spin round in a waltz, oh, what a delight!
They toss all their colors, a crimson parade,
While squirrels join in with a fast-paced charade.

The crisp air is filled with a tickle and laugh,
As pumpkins debate who's the finest by half.
One claims to be king, with a crown carved in lace,
While the others just grin, it's a ridiculous race.

A crow with a monocle caws down the lane,
Demanding respect like a pompous refrain.
Yet one fluttering leaf gives a cheeky response,
And a gust of pure mischief starts the whole jaunt!

So let's sway to the tunes of this autumnal flurry,
With twirls and with whirls, and just a hint of curry.
The last dance begins, with a huff and a pout,
As all of the forest spins round and about!

Fortunes Beneath the Underbrush

A hedgehog with goggles, oh what a surprise,
Scours the soft soil for a treasure that lies.
He digs with a grin, but just finds a shoe,
And ponders if fashion's a fortune too.

A mole starts to bother, with dreams of a plot,
"What I need is a hat!" he squeaks with great thought.
He rummages through with a flourish and flair,
Uncovering bugs! Oh, the gourmet affair!

A rabbit sells maps to the lost and confused,
"Follow me quick! You won't be bemused!"
But what's really here is a stash of old grass,
He chuckles aloud as they pass it on past.

So fortune or folly, who really can say?
In the underbrush laughter will always hold sway.
So grab up your shovel, dig deep, take a chance,
You might just unearth a wild woodland dance!

The Unraveling of Quiet Melodies

In the hush of the night, a mouse with a flute,
Played tunes on a whim, oh sweet little brute!
But a cat with a grin, prowling near by,
Joined in with his voice, such a cheeky sly guy.

The fireflies blinked like they owned the show,
Dancing to rhythms that nobody knows.
A chorus of crickets chimed in the fun,
While shadows grew larger, and better begun.

The wind caught the notes, swirled them around,
Carried laughter and merry, a whimsical sound.
Yet just in a moment, the music took flight,
And everyone questioned, "Is that wrong or right?"

So let's spin and twirl to our own silly beats,
With critters and creatures, we dance on our feet.
In the unraveling night, laughter fills the air,
As melodies whisper, wild and unfair!

Reveries of the Overgrown Trail.

In tangled vines, a squirrel stuck,
A fussing, flapping ball of luck.
He chirps about his hazel stash,
While branches swing in wild, green thrash.

A thump and a bump, then giggles ensue,
A raccoon sneezes—what a hullabaloo!
The ferns around begin to sway,
As bears join in the forest play.

A porcupine juggles acorns galore,
While owls watch, their eyes wide, wanting more.
In muddy puddles, we all leap,
Chasing shadows that giggle, then creep.

The path may twist like a kaleidoscope,
Yet laughter blooms with each little hope.
In the riotous green, we can't help but grin,
For adventure waits where the stories begin.

In the Heart of Untamed Grief

A rabbit laments his lost lettuce leaf,
With dramatic flair, he channels his grief.
In floppy ears and a heart that quakes,
He dances silly, for laughter he makes.

A deer flips over a branch, takes a fall,
While squirrels gather to laugh at it all.
Together they build a throne of pine,
For those who stumble, it's just divine.

The wind whispers secrets, a giggle or two,
While fireflies giggle, twinkling like dew.
In the heart of these woes, mirth isn't shy,
For every fond fumble, we twirl and we fly.

So if you should find, in sorrow a bite,
Just look for the critters dancing in light.
With chuckles and cheer, they'll show you the way,
Through all of life's woes, come laugh and play.

Whispering Shadows and Starlit Dreams

The shadows flicker like a disco ball,
As night critters gather for the grand call.
A centipede twirls in a silly parade,
While moonbeams sprinkle a glimmering cascade.

A badger shimmies, declaring it's fun,
With antics and dances until the sun.
A chorus of crickets joins in the sound,
In this woodland rave, we're all tightly bound.

A firefly wipes off the dust of the day,
While raccoons trade stories, both silly and gay.
Who needs a bed when the stars shine bright?
Together we frolic and dance through the night.

In shadows and dreams, our laughter takes flight,
We'd rather be foolish than serious tonight.
With joy echoing deep in the rustling leaves,
The whispers of wonder are all that we need.

The Echoes of Rustling Leaves

Beneath the trees, a chatty crowd,
With whispers that giggle, shy and loud.
A wild chipmunk sparks crazy debates,
While all the wise owls just roll their states.

The leaves are rustling some secret code,
As foxes dance in a comical mode.
One tumbles down into a patch of dirt,
Poking fun at the dread of getting hurt.

A woodpecker's rap is a funky beat,
While squirrels get down, showing off their feet.
Beneath it all, laughter does weave,
In echoes of fun that the trees believe.

So join in the joy, in the rustle and cheer,
For nature's sweet folly is perfectly clear.
With every sweet giggle and joyful refrain,
The woods come alive, never feeling the pain.

Songs of the Whispering Winds

Through branches wide, the breezes hum,
Leaves gossip tales, oh what a fun!
A squirrel forgot his nutty treat,
Chasing shadows on tiny feet.

The old tree laughs, it shakes its bark,
Rustling whispers, a merry lark.
A wandering deer, caught in a jest,
Buckles and stumbles, it's not the best.

In this lively grove, all creatures sing,
Nature's comedy, an endless fling.
Roaming raccoons, masks on their face,
Stealing snacks with such silly grace.

Thus, winds carry giggles, soft and light,
In this funny forest, pure delight.
Among the laughs, we find our way,
In the woodland gaiety, we play.

The Lost Path Amongst the Ferns

Once I took that path of green,
Thought I was clever, a walking dream.
But ferns, they laughed, 'You shouldn't roam!'
Each step I took led me far from home.

A rabbit chirped, 'You're quite a sight!'
Lost among greens, oh what a plight!
I tripped on roots, fell flat with flair,
Now I'm the talk of the woodland fair.

Mice twirled 'round, a dance so spry,
With thumping paws they said, 'Oh my!'
A hedgehog winked and rolled on by,
'You'll find your way, just don't you cry!'

In trailing ferns where laughter's found,
I learned the woods twist joy around.
Each lost adventure's a story spun,
In giggles shared, we all have fun.

Heartbeats of the Ancient Oak

Oh mighty oak, with arms so wide,
You cradle secrets, where critters hide.
A woodpecker's knock, it's a quirky beat,
Tapping a rhythm, oh what a feat!

Squirrels in suits, they scamper and tease,
Planning their heists with mischievous ease.
Branch to branch, in chaotic dance,
Life in the canopy, a wild romance.

Under your branches, tales intertwine,
Of acorns lost and old vines that twine.
A raccoon rolls in a leaf pile's glee,
Spreading the laughter like roots of a tree.

Through seasons changing, you stand so proud,
Guarding the fun in a green-capped shroud.
With heartbeats echoing in every bough,
You remind us to laugh, here and now.

The Dance of Flickering Fireflies

In twilight's hush, they spark and twirl,
Little lights in a night-time swirl.
Fireflies winking, a dazzling show,
Lighting up paths where the wild winds blow.

Gathering round, the crickets' cheer,
In this glow, all troubles disappear.
With flicks and flares they start their play,
Chasing shadows 'til the break of day.

One slipped and tumbled, oh what a spin!
Landing near me with a giggle and grin.
"I think I'm dizzy!" it blinked with glee,
As we laughed together, just wild and free.

So here in the dark, with friends alight,
We dance and frolic, oh what a sight!
Nature's tiny jesters, bright and bold,
In their enchanting dance, joy unfolds.

Prism of the Hidden Glens

In the glen where shadows dwell,
A toad wears shoes—not quite swell.
He hops around, a jolly sight,
Singing songs both day and night.

A squirrel with glasses reads the news,
While raccoons debate their fashion muse.
Amidst the laughter, it seems quite clear,
The forest folk hold humor dear.

A bear in a tutu joins the fun,
While ants prepare a race to run.
With giggles echoing through the trees,
They dance and twirl, all at their ease.

Oh, the mischief woven in each twig,
From grouchy owls to chirpy twig.
In the prism of color, joy they share,
Life's a circus—who could compare?

Murmurs of the Sylvan Heart

Amidst the leaves, a chatter forms,
With rabbits telling all their charms.
A hedgehog's tale of bravest flight,
Makes all the critters squeal with delight.

Foxes dangle from a bough,
Claiming crowns—they're kings, somehow!
A chattering parrot gives a nod,
As the voices rise like a cheerful sod.

The tree trunks giggle, roots do shake,
As porcupines bake a pie mistake.
The squirrels cheer, "It's not our fault!"
When one takes a tumble in a vault.

Murmurs of laughter fill the air,
In a heart where joy is bare.
From tales untold to songs of cheer,
Laughter spreads all far and near.

Reflections in the Dew-kissed Dawn

In morning's light, the dew drops glint,
A ladybug dons a mischievous hint.
She rides a snail with grand aplomb,
While the world around begins to hum.

A frog in a crown sings opera loud,
While crickets gather, feeling proud.
They boast of the party from last night,
With tales of dance and slight fright.

Golden rays peek shyly through,
While bees pursue their morning brew.
A butterfly trips, lands on a paw,
Of a sleep-tangled cat—oh, what a flaw!

Reflections sparkle, life's a game,
Each dawn unfolds a brand new name.
With laughter echoed in each glade,
The beauty of morning never does fade.

Fables from the Fern-laden Paths

Along the path where ferns do grow,
A fox tells tales of an old crow.
She wears a hat, it's not quite right,
A sight that brings the stars to light.

A partridge claims a velvet throne,
With tales of bravery widely sown.
While rabbits roll in clover's bloom,
Creating laughs that chase away gloom.

A badger in overalls cooks a stew,
Adding spices he found—quite a few!
With every bite, the guests all cheer,
For fables bring warmth, and smiles are sheer.

From fern-laden paths to skies above,
Each tale is sprinkled with wild love.
In the forest's embrace, they find delight,
In the stories shared, day turns to night.

Raindrops on Forgotten Paths

Puddles gather in my shoes,
With every step, I sing the blues.
The trees above start to dance,
While squirrels feast—a nutty chance.

Umbrellas flip, they take to flight,
As winds join in, a wild delight.
A slippery business, this old trek,
I think I'll stick to sitting—heck!

High above, a chorus of caws,
Distracted by the wet ground's flaws.
It's hard to walk, so let's just slip,
Each raindrop feels like a playful quip.

But through the drizzles, laughter peeks,
In muddy boots, we'll dance like freaks.
Though soaked and stuck, we don't despair,
For every splash brings joys to share.

The Lament of the Hidden Stream

In shadows deep, the waters hide,
With giggles soft, they slip and glide.
A pebble's toss, a splashy sound,
Makes fishy tales all the more profound.

But frogs croak loud, oh what a mess,
Their symphony, I must confess.
They croon of bugs and long-lost flies,
While dragonflies roll their tiny eyes.

Beneath the rush, a rumor brews,
They plot and plan, a silly ruse.
To hop and skip, their legs all strong,
To dance the night, their hearts belong.

Yet in the silence, old grass leans,
Listening close to silly scenes.
The hidden stream, with whispers weaves,
In laughter's depths, the heart believes.

Murmurs of the Woodland Spirit

Oh playful winds, they twist and twirl,
The leaves do laugh, and nuts unfurl.
A sprite peeks out from bark's embrace,
With cheeky grins, it wins the race.

A rustle here, a giggle there,
Twirling 'round without a care.
The mushrooms bob their tiny heads,
As branches dance, and laughter spreads.

"Come join the fun!" the spirit cries,
While faeries wink with sparkling eyes.
In every nook, where shadows creep,
The mischief hides, the woods asleep.

So heed their calls, don't run away,
For woodland whims are here to stay.
In chortles lost, with nature's swirl,
You'll find the joy that makes you whirl.

A Soliloquy in the Glen

In the glen, where daisies sway,
The bumblebees begin to play.
A gentle hum, a zany song,
Where all the quirky critters throng.

"Who's in charge?" asks a bright-eyed mouse,
As hedgehogs giggle in the house.
A snail debates the fastest route,
While ants just march, without a doubt.

But lo! A stumble, who could it be?
A raccoon tripped—oh joy, oh glee!
He shakes his paws, now what a sight,
With berries stuck, a comical plight.

Yet as the sun begins to set,
The woodland banter we won't forget.
In laughter's grip, as shadows creep,
The glen will sing us off to sleep.

The Hidden Color of Grief

In the forest, a raccoon is bold,
Wearing my hat, so gleefully told.
He struts through the trees with a laugh and a twirl,
While squirrels are snickering, giving a whirl.

The brook gurgles on with a splash and a cheer,
A fish jumps out, saying, "Who's next in here?"
It steals my sandwich, then dives out of sight,
Leaving me hungry, yet still feeling bright.

The shadowy paths hide strange little things,
Like frogs in top hats, and birds made of springs.
They dance in the twilight, a comedic scene,
While rabbits write scripts for a show yet unseen.

So laughter echoes through each tangled branch,
As I trip over roots and give fate a chance.
The tears may flow, but they come with a grin,
In this jolly forest, where all troubles thin.

Echoes of Lush Desolation

A parrot squawks gossip from high on a beam,
Spilling the secrets of the old willow's dream.
"That tree once had leaves, but now it's a stick,"
It cackles in laughter, as if it's a trick.

The groundhogs gather, they plot and they scheme,
To snatch away cookies from the campfire's gleam.
"They're fighting again, those pesky young deer!"
Squeaks a mouse wearing socks with a look of sheer cheer.

The bark is alive with chatter and cheer,
While the owls tell tales that no one can hear.
With vines that entangle and thorns that tease,
Each wanderer stumbles, and humor's the breeze.

Though shadows may loom in this forest of twine,
The laughter's contagious, as we all intertwine.
In the rustling branches, the giggles are wild,
For out here in nature, we're all just a child.

The Enigma of the Elder's Whispers

An old tree once claimed it could tell me a joke,
But all that it made were roots made of smoke.
"I cracked up a worm, that creature once cried,"
It chuckled with pride, as it stretched out wide.

The owls, they hoot in their robes of fine mist,
Reciting old stories, they insist we can't miss.
But their punchlines are flat and their rhythm is slow,
As the hedgehogs roll in, all covered in woe.

A chipmunk with style struts like a queen,
"I once danced with fireflies, it was quite the scene!"
Yet in her high heels, she slips 'neath the ferns,
While butterflies giggle and adjust their concerns.

In the wisdom of trees, we gather our glee,
For laughter is just as important as tea.
So we sip on the echoes that ring through the vale,
With whispers of humor that never grow stale.

Love Letters to the Unvisited Glade

A clearing so bright, yet no one can find,
Where ferns hold their secrets and shadows unwind.
A raccoon writes poems with berries and glee,
He sends them to stars that twinkle agreeably.

The toads hold a meeting on rocks made of moss,
Discussing their outfits, no matter the cost.
"If I wear this hat, will it bring me more flies?"
And the gossip that follows is quite the surprise.

The flowers all giggle at bees' clumsy dance,
As they drop all their nectar, and lose their romance.
With petals in disarray, color spills free,
In this untouched glade, where chaos helps thee.

So pen little letters to places unknown,
For each silly moment is laughter we've sown.
In glades lost to time, fun echoes and swells,
As critters compose all their whimsical spells.

Chronicles of the Fading Trail

A raccoon sat on a log, quite proud,
With chips on his face, he looked out loud.
He claimed to be king of the forgotten way,
But tripped on a root and fell in dismay.

The squirrels held court with their acorn stash,
While birds chirped loudly, a colorful bash.
They voted on snacks for the feast that night,
But forgot the rules, oh, what a silly plight!

Old maples debated on who's still the best,
While ferns rolled their eyes, not caring the jest.
Their laughter echoed through branches so wide,
As pine trees whispered secrets, side by side.

The Thorns of Forgotten Trails

A hedgehog strolled with a thistle in tow,
It pricked at his side but he didn't quite know.
He puffed out his chest, "I'm a warrior bold!"
Then stumbled on thorns and turned quickly cold.

The old fox was clever, with tricks up his sleeve,
He conjured up tales that no one believed.
But when he wore boots, tripped over his paws,
The laughter erupted, and no one gave pause.

The brambles conspired to tangle and tease,
While beetles played poker on bumps of rough leaves.
They rolled up the dice made of acorn caps,
And placed tiny bets for the next round of laughs.

Flickers of Hope in the Brambles

A rabbit named Bob had a habit to brag,
Of winning the races with a speedy zigzag.
But mystified by brambles, he lost his cool,
And found himself stuck, oh what a fool!

The deer had been scheming, quite fond of the chase,
While frogs made a ruckus, enjoying the space.
A reminder that life's not just about speed,
Sometimes you stop for a flower or seed.

The fireflies danced with a flicker so bright,
While crickets provided the tune for the night.
Bob, with a grin, now a part of the show,
Learned laughter's a treasure, as wild breezes blow.

Amidst Ruins of Ancient Boughs

Two owls discussing their grand, old demise,
Claimed wisdom from age, yet rolled their own eyes.
They hooted of tales from the nights long ago,
While hiding from daylight, avoiding the show.

A porcupine puffed up, determined and brave,
He swore he could dance, though he swayed like a wave.
But the birds couldn't stop their giggles and chortles,
As he spun round and round, bumping into the portals.

A mistletoe party, all awkward and bright,
With love at a distance, pure joy in the fright.
Yet whispers of friendship sung sweet from the trees,
As laughter took flight on a joyful breeze.

Beneath the Twisting Branches

Beneath the twisting branches high,
The squirrels plot, oh me, oh my.
They hoard the acorns, big and small,
Laughing at humans who trip and fall.

The shadows whisper jokes so sly,
While crickets chirp a lullaby.
A rabbit sneezes — oh dear, what fun!
And all the deer join in the run!

Who knew that life could twist so well,
In this leafy, green, enchanted swell?
With mossy shoes and laughter loud,
The forest holds a hilarity shroud.

So come, dear friends, take a leap,
Join the wood folks in a merry sweep.
From tree to tree, we'll all partake,
In silly games that nature makes.

Secrets of the Thicket

In thickets thick, where shadows dance,
A raccoon wears a sneaky glance.
With shiny eyes and paws so quick,
He steals a snack — oh what a trick!

The bushes speak in riddles old,
As brambles tangle stories told.
A beetle struts with fancied flair,
While mice play tag without a care.

A lizard winks from sunlit stone,
His buddy's lost — he's all alone.
A wise old owl, with beard of gray,
Cackles at all who lose their way.

So heed the tales the bushes spin,
With every splash of laughter's din.
For in this thicket, strange and bright,
You'll find your joy in every fright.

The Dance of the Lost Fern

A fern in frolic, lost in glee,
Did a jig and spun with thee.
With fronds a-flutter, not a care,
It tripped on roots, oh what a scare!

The groundhog winked and joined the spree,
While flowers giggled 'neath a tree.
Each step a tumble, a bumble and sway,
Creating chaos in the sun's ray.

Tokens of laughter filled the air,
As nature rejoiced in splendid flair.
The ferns were twirling with utter delight,
In this whimsical waltz through day and night.

So watch for the dance, but be aware,
The forest floor can lead to despair.
Yet for all the blunders and slips we earn,
The spirit of laughter is what we learn.

Solitude Among Ancient Trees

Amidst the giants, I find my wits,
With nudges from squirrels and clever bits.
A conifer chuckles, its branches wide,
While the oaks hold secrets, with pride they bide.

A whispered joke from roots below,
While branches spread their tales of woe.
The winds will howl and often sigh,
As critters dance and the shadows lie.

Alone I linger, yet not for long,
For nature's chorus hums a song.
The hoot of an owl, the croak of a frog,
Turn solitude into a playful dialogue.

Among these ancients, oh what bliss,
A tapestry of mirth, I can't dismiss.
Embrace the quirks, the jests so free,
In solemn woods, there's comedy!

Shadows Amidst the Blooming

In the garden, a snail took his time,
Wearing a hat made of lime.
A squirrel debated on eating a shoe,
While bees danced a jig, oblivious to you.

Flowers giggled under the sun,
Each petal a joke, each stem just for fun.
A butterfly fluffed up her bright wings,
And told of her travels on wild-faring things.

But shadows will gather when laughter's too loud,
A sneaky raccoon, the garden's sworn shroud.
He swiped some snacks and dashed out of sight,
Leaving the flowers to ponder all night.

The day ended merrily, spirits were high,
In a meandering row, the daisies did sigh.
For every sweet moment hides a small jest,
Amidst blossoms and blooms, life surely is blessed.

The Roots of Regret

Beneath the surface, where secrets do dwell,
Tree roots whisper stories, too funny to tell.
A carrot once boasted of digging so deep,
Till a worm poked his head out, and caused a great leap.

Regretting his comments, the carrot turned red,
While a gopher just laughed, spinning tales in his bed.
"I'm the king of the soil!" the carrot did claim,
But the worm burrowed deeper, amused by the game.

An acorn tooted its horn, proud as can be,
Until a gust of wind set it tumbling, you see.
The roots of their laughter intertwined so tight,
Regrets became giggles, under pale moonlight.

From underground kingdom, the chuckles arose,
As each little creature embraced all their woes.
In the dark earth's embrace, comedy finds,
That roots full of laughter can often unwind.

Secrets Woven in Green

In the tall grass, a secret was spun,
A mouse told a tale, just for fun.
With leaves whispering words that tickled the breeze,
Every thistle held secrets, guarded with ease.

A hedgehog ambling, his quills in a fuss,
Claimed he was famous for riding a bus!
But the bus was a leaf, and the ride was a slide,
Yet all of his friends giggled, bursting with pride.

A chatty chameleon changed colors with glee,
"I've seen things you humans could never foresee!"
But tripped on a branch while trying to boast,
And landed in laughter, the naturefolk's host.

Amidst woven tales, in shades of bright green,
Lives a laughable world, where quirks are routine.
For every odd twist, and secret untold,
Is a story that's waiting, just ready to unfold.

Beneath the Cover of Verdant Canopies

Under thick branches, the critters convene,
Where laughter erupts and joy reigns serene.
A raccoon in pajamas, quite lost in his dream,
Found himself napping on a strange-looking beam.

The owls exchanged looks, all puzzled and wise,
As one told a joke that brought tears to their eyes.
"Why did the squirrel climb so high on that tree?"
"To get to the nut shop – now doesn't that spree?"

The laughter echoed through pockets of shade,
While a woodpecker's drumming perfectly played.
A turtle joined in, with a slow little spin,
Saying, "I'll be the judge—let the fun now begin!"

Beneath the green cover, where giggles combine,
Each critter found solace in whimsical rhyme.
For in the end, what is life but a jest,
When surrounded by friends, we are surely blessed.

A Tempest Among the Saplings

A gust swirled, the branches danced,
A bird flew by, it barely pranced.
With acorns flying like cannonballs,
The little squirrel just laughs and sprawls.

A twig snapped off, the trees all shook,
A raccoon peeked out from a nook.
"Who's causing all this ruckus here?"
The foliage whispered, "Never fear!"

The winds proclaimed a game of tag,
Where pinecones flew like a crazy brag.
The bushes rustled in joyful glee,
Nature's laughter was wild and free.

As storms rolled through, chaos reigned,
Yet every critter remained unchained.
They danced around with all their might,
In a tempest that felt just right!

Chronicles of the Wandering Breeze

Oh, the breeze that roams so wide,
Tickling leaves, with joy and pride.
It tugged a hat right off a head,
Leaving a giggle where once dread.

A swaying branch said, "Look at me!"
"I'm doing tricks, come see, come see!"
With every twist and tiny whirl,
The wildflowers danced, giving a twirl.

Bugs flew high on this zephyr ride,
Chasing each other, side by side.
But then the grass took hold and gripped,
A ladybug who surely slipped!

Yet with a pop, they all were free,
Laughing wildly, oh what glee!
The breeze just giggled, spun around,
In nature's chaos, joy is found.

Tapestry of Forgotten Trails

In the woods where shadows creep,
Old paths linger, secrets keep.
A raccoon stumbles, quite the sight,
His clumsy prance brings pure delight.

Amidst the leaves, a story's spun,
Of paths once walked by everyone.
Yet here comes a badger, sly and stout,
He trips on roots and gives a shout!

Moths flutter by, with grace they drift,
While bushes giggle at the mishift.
"Why use the path when you can leap?"
One squirrel chortled, "It's all a heap!"

The journey's wild, adventures abound,
With every twist, laughter is found.
In this land of trails and jests,
Nature shows her very best.

Lullabies of the Ancient Earth

Underneath the starry cloak,
A worm hums soft, with every stroke.
The crickets play their soothing tune,
Beneath the watchful, smiling moon.

Yet wait! A hedgehog's nightly quest,
With tiny feet, he tries his best.
He bumps a root, then offers a squeal,
Making every creature's mirth reveal.

The owls hoot, with wise surprise,
As fireflies blink like tiny eyes.
"Not so fast!" says a beetle bold,
"Let's race around till stories unfold!"

As night stretches on, tales are spun,
In this sleepy wood, all in fun.
Though nature gently sings her song,
It's full of giggles, all night long.

Beneath the Echoing Canopy

In the forest where squirrels debate,
Their acorns get used for a bumpy fate.
Trees wear masks made of leaves so bright,
Chasing shadows that dance in the light.

A raccoon runs off with a shiny spoon,
Whispers to owls about the moon.
Mushrooms wear hats, quite stylish and bold,
While the forest giggles at secrets untold.

Beneath the echo, the echoes collide,
As daisies complain of thorns they can't hide.
The sunbeams tumble, tickling the ground,
Here in this realm, such nonsense abound.

Oh, what a place where critters all sing,
Lamenting the weight of a butterfly's wing.
Nature's oddities, each tale a delight,
Beneath the canopy, smiles take flight.

A Haven of Silent Despair

In a glade where the lost rabbits fret,
They seek out the hats of a fox named set.
The lilies gossip, their whispers are hushed,
While a worm in the soil feels ever so rushed.

Cardinals plot with a cheeky old crow,
On sunny days laughing beneath winds that blow.
The breeze tells secrets most silly and grand,
Yet the mushrooms sigh with their heads in the sand.

Ferns frantically dance to the tune of the flies,
Hiding the truth with a well-crafted disguise.
In a haven of silence, the whispers are still,
But tumbleweeds rolling bring a laughter to fill.

The petals provide the most colorful shade,
Where chubby toads sing of the dreams that they made.
This place may seem lost, without hope, or flair,
Yet giggles erupt in the silent despair.

Nature's Unwritten Chronicles

Beneath the twist of the bramble and vine,
Ants march with purpose in an awkward line.
Grasshoppers grumble, their songs out of tune,
While bumblebees twirl like they're tipsy at noon.

The tales of the trees whisper loud and clear,
Of giggles and mischief from far and near.
A porcupine knitting with threads of sharp pride,
Sews patches of laughter where lost thoughts reside.

Bugs have their meetings, discussing the buzz,
While fungi throw parties, just because they can fuzz.
Each petal is dancing, wrapped in its hue,
Creating a world full of whimsical view.

Nature's own tales become legends to weave,
Of critters who trick and just never believe.
In the stories we find, oh, the wonder and cheer,
Of laughter that echoes throughout the year.

The Twilight's Call to the Lost

When the dim light softens at the end of the day,
The shadows stretch long, in a humorous way.
Fireflies giggle, as they flicker and glow,
Whispers of nonsense as they put on a show.

The moon's got a grin, with a twinkle that sings,
While raccoons dance 'round with their shiny new bling.
With nighttime attire, they shuffle and prance,
Mistakenly thinking it's all just a dance.

A deer pulls a face at a passing old frog,
As he croaks out a tune 'neath the sprawling fog.
They humor the owls with peculiar tales,
Of llamas in pajamas and snails wearing veils.

In twilight's sweet call, the strange gathers round,
In a place full of giggles, where joy can be found.
Lost in their laughter, what a merry display,
As nature unravels in the dusk's gentle sway.

Hidden Sorrows in the Understory

Beneath the leaves, a squirrel frets,
His acorn stash, a source of debts.
A grumpy raccoon, with a hat askew,
Counts his treasures, but can't find two.

The mushrooms giggle under the gloom,
While snails slide past with thoughts of doom.
A toadstool's sigh, a fuzzy bug's cheer,
Each whisper dances, loud and clear.

But no one knows of the lurking plight,
The snickering ferns, they bloom at night.
With wild, wild tales, they spin and weave,
Hidden worries, no one believes.

So here's to the woods, where grief is shy,
And laughter winks beneath the sky.
For in each shadow, a jest does lie,
Among the leaves, flutters a tiny sigh.

Eternal Vigil of the Elder Tree

Stretched high and wide, the elder grins,
Counting the knots where the fun begins.
A bevy of birds, in coats of bright hue,
Tell secrets of squirrels, and elder's fond view.

But what's to be done with a bark so wise?
It scolds the ants and their tiny lies.
The roots do chuckle, as breezes tease,
While old Mr. Owl naps with ease.

A chipmunk's dance, a porcupine's frown,
Leaves rustle softly as they spin round.
With branches like arms, elder waves back,
To the skittering creatures on their wild track.

Through timeless giggles and playful jests,
The elder endures, passing all tests.
But like every sage, with wisdom to share,
He hides in the laughter, with all of us there.

Whispers of a Healing Breeze

A gentle breeze tickles the tufts of grass,
While trees tell tales of a sassy sass.
With a rustling giggle, it sings to the leaves,
Spinning stories no one believes.

A butterfly flutters, in spots of delight,
Dancing with shadows, till leaping at night.
Laughter echoes from bluejay's call,
As winds weave through branches, a whimsical sprawl.

The rocks hold whispers of giggling streams,
While troughs of water play in dream beams.
"Oh dear!" says a pebble, with a wink to the sun,
"No glum little gravel shall dampen our fun!"

The breeze nudges flowers to sway and sway,
As laughter spreads through the light of the day.
With every hush, it finds its way,
In rustles and chuckles, all spirits play.

The Mask of the Wandering Haze

In the misty morn, a creature peeks,
Dressed in a fog, with ticklish cheeks.
With a wink and a grin, it drifts on by,
Who needs a map when the giggles fly?

A raccoon with flair tips its hat to the cloud,
While mushrooms below get slightly too loud.
"I swear I heard jokes from a nearby tree,"
"Or maybe that was just a cheeky bee!"

The shadows dance in a playful chase,
As the fog rolls on through the underbrush space.
Leaves flutter softly, with mischief afoot,
And the mask of the haze gives a sneaky salute.

So laugh with the mist, let the stories bloom,
For every nook hides a giggle or two.
As the world spins by with a humorous twirl,
May the haze bring joy to each little swirl.

The Burden of Overgrown Trails

I tripped on a root, my shoes went flying,
My dignity faded, oh, why was I trying?
A vine wrapped my leg, it waltzed me around,
In this tangled mess, no rescue is found.

The bushes are laughing, I swear they can talk,
With branches that giggle as I do the walk.
A squirrel snickers, it's quite the parade,
In this leafy circus, my confidence fades.

Each turn leads to chaos, a thicket of fun,
A labyrinth waiting, here I come undone!
I thought I was brave, but now I just pout,
These overgrown trails have me figuring out.

It's a slapstick escapade drenched in green,
With laughter in nature, oh, what a scene!
The forest is wild, but it loves a good jest,
As I tumble and stumble, I must jest with the best.

Songs of the Moonlit Grove

In a grove under stars, the crickets compose,
A symphony sweet, but discard their clothes!
The owl hoots a rhythm, it's all quite absurd,
As fireflies dance, oh, how they've stirred!

The raccoons have joined, they're stealing the show,
With tambourines made of acorns in tow.
The moon beams its smile, but giggles instead,
As each little critter joins in with their head.

A fox claims the mic, but forgot all the words,
His jokes feel like feathers, light as the birds.
The shadows are howling, a comical sight,
In this moonlit soirée, all worries take flight.

With laughter and music, the night seems to cheer,
Nature's own tale, it's the funniest year!
As I watch the wild antics, my heart starts to soar,
In the songs of the grove, I couldn't ask for more.

Memories Carved in Bark

I found a tree that's scribbled my tale,
With hearts and some arrows - oh, how bold they unveil!
The carvings in bark, they dance and they prance,
Each scratch tells a story of love and a chance.

An 'A + B' where the laughter unfurled,
Is now an 'A + whoops' in this whimsical world.
I traced all the lines, now I'm lost in the past,
Missed my own dinner, this joy is too fast!

The squirrels take notes, with eyes full of glee,
They plan a new tale, a sequel for me.
With each little knot, they plot and they scheme,
A saga of silliness, a wild tree dream.

Every mark on that trunk brings a chuckle or two,
In the forest, it seems, I've found my own crew.
They gather 'round closely, oh, I can't help but smile,
With memories carved, I'm stuck here awhile.

Cascading Thoughts in Twisted Vines

Tangled in thought and oh my, what a mess,
 A whirlwind of musings, I must confess.
The vines twist around like my brain in a knot,
Nature's own jester, I'm caught in the plot.

As leaves whisper secrets, the sun starts to grin,
My worries lie dormant; I'm arm wrestling win.
The branches wave hello while I ponder away,
Each decision I make seems to waltz and betray.

A flower's advice comes in colors so bright,
"Just let go!" it shouts, "you'll be fine, take a flight!"
So I giggle at troubles, like they're jesters in line,
With laughter entwined in these cascading vines.

Each thought is a treasure, though jumbled and wild,
Through nature's embrace, I feel carefree like a child.
In this garden of whimsy, my heart takes its chance,
As I twirl with the vines, oh, come join in the dance.

Cries Beneath the Canopy

In the trees a squirrel squeaks,
Chasing dreams and crispy peaks.
A raccoon stumbles, slips and falls,
While a wise old owl just calmly sprawls.

Frogs in chorus singing loud,
Croaking tunes, drawing a crowd.
Bumblebees with sticky charm,
Buzz around, no cause for alarm.

A fox slips by, a stealthy creep,
On his tail, a rabbit leaps.
Laughter echoes through the leaves,
Nature's comedy, or so it weaves.

With hidden giggles in the air,
Every critter shows they care.
In this realm of lush delight,
Every mishap is pure insight.

Fragments of Sunlight on the Forest Floor

Sunbeams dance on leafy beds,
Lighting up the paths where tread.
A chipmunk darts with nuts to hoard,
While a turtle just wants to afford.

Dappled light upon the ground,
Footprints of creatures all around.
A rabbit prances, full of glee,
Underneath the shade of a big tree.

The show-off deer prances about,
Too proud, it makes the others pout.
A stumpy toad just wants to bask,
In sunshine's glow, that's all it asks.

Mushrooms giggle, tickled by rays,
Winking at the sunlight's plays.
With each beam, a chuckle stirs,
Nature's jokes without the slurs.

Shadows Longing for the Light

Shadows creep where fireflies gleam,
Hiding secrets in their dream.
A grumpy raccoon yawns out loud,
Wishing for stars in the gloomy shroud.

Silly mice in a midnight rush,
Tiptoe softly, oh what a hush!
A bold little bat zooms by,
Chasing shadows as they fly.

The moonlight tickles all around,
While sleepy owls hoot a sound.
A playful breeze, a gentle tease,
Makes the night dance with quirky ease.

Echoes of laughter in the dark,
Nature's spark, a cheeky lark.
As the shadows stretch with grace,
They carve out fun in their embrace.

A Tapestry of Unseen Struggles

In the thicket, whispers blend,
A snicker here, a chuckle's end.
A hedgehog rolls to ease its woes,
While a deer stumbles, oh how it goes!

Branches creak with tales untold,
Adventures woven, bright and bold.
A caterpillar tries to crawl,
Dreaming of wings, to rise with all.

The chipmunk's stash is running low,
While the rabbit hops to steal the show.
With every step, a slip or two,
In this jungle, a hoot and a moo!

Yet through the trials, laughter rings,
Nature's way of giving wings.
Through unseen struggles, a path so bright,
In the tapestry, joy takes flight.

www.ingramcontent.com/pod-product-compliance
Lightning Source LLC
Chambersburg PA
CBHW071846160426
43209CB00003B/442